Raccoons

by L. Patricia Kite
photographs by Jerry Boucher

Lerner Publications Company • Minneapolis, Minnesota

To Leslie, Elinor and Isabelle, cousins and best friends
—LPK

Additional photographs are reproduced through the courtesy of: p. 7 © Jack Milchanowski/
Visuals Unlimited; pp. 8, 19, 26, 28, 34, 41 © Leonard Rue Enterprises/Leonard Lee Rue III;
p. 17 © R. Al Simpson/Visuals Unlimited; p. 29 © Steve Maslowski/Visuals Unlimited; pp. 33,
38, 42 © Leonard Rue Enterprises/Len Rue, Jr.; p. 36 © R. Lindholm/Visuals Unlimited.

Text copyright ©2004 by L. Patricia Kite

Photographs copyright © 2004 by Lerner Publications Company, except as noted.

Website address: www.lernerbooks.com

Lerner Publications Company
A division of Lerner Publishing Group
241 First Avenue North
Minneapolis, Minnesota 55401 U.S.A.

Library of Congress Cataloging-in-Publication Data

Kite, L. Patricia.
     Raccoons / by L. Patricia Kite ; photographs by Jerry Boucher.
        p.   cm. — (Early bird nature books)
     Summary: An introduction to the physical characteristics,
  behavior, habitat, and life cycle of raccoons.
     ISBN: 0-8225-3049-X (lib. bdg. : alk. paper)
     1. Raccoons—Juvenile literature. [1. Raccoons.] I. Boucher,
  Jerry, 1941– ill. II. Title. III. Series.
  QL737.C26 K58 2004
  599.76'32—dc21   2002010675

Manufactured in the United States of America
1 2 3 4 5 6 – JR – 09 08 07 06 05 04

Contents

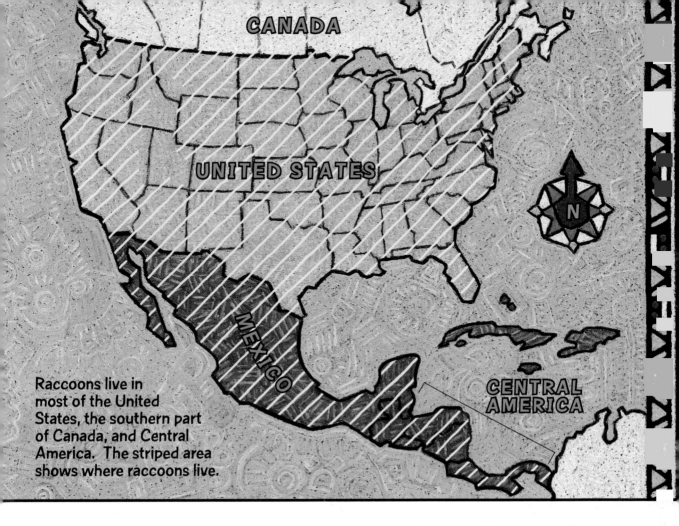

CANADA

UNITED STATES

N

MEXICO

CENTRAL AMERICA

Raccoons live in most of the United States, the southern part of Canada, and Central America. The striped area shows where raccoons live.

Be a Word Detective

Can you find these words as you read about the raccoon's life? Be a detective and try to figure out what they mean. You can turn to the glossary on page 46 for help.

dens	**home range**	**omnivores**
forefeet	**kits**	**predators**
guard hairs	**nocturnal**	**underfur**

Chapter 1

The common raccoon has several names. It can be called the northern raccoon. Or it can be called the North American raccoon. Where do common raccoons live?

The Clever Raccoon

 Raccoons are very curious. They like to explore new places. They like to touch new things. And they are very clever.

There are two main species, or kinds, of raccoons. One species is called the crab-eating raccoon. It lives in Central America and South America. The other species is called the common raccoon. It lives in the southern part of Canada, most of the United States, and Central America. This book is about the common raccoon.

Common raccoons may live in places that have cold temperatures.

Raccoons are closely related to ringtails, coatis (kuh-WAHT-eez), and kinkajous (KING-kuh-joohz). Some scientists think raccoons are also related to red pandas.

Ringtails and raccoons look much alike.

The common raccoon's scientific name is Procyon lotor.

An adult raccoon usually weighs 12 to 30 pounds. This is about as heavy as a large watermelon. Raccoons are 2 to 3 feet long from their nose to the end of their tail. This is about as long as a baseball bat. Male raccoons are usually bigger than female raccoons.

Most of a raccoon's fur is brown, gray, black, or yellowish. Raccoons have two types of fur. Most of their fur is underfur. Underfur is short, thick, and warm. Raccoons also have longer hairs called guard (GAHRD) hairs. Raccoons have long, bushy tails. A raccoon's tail has five to seven black stripes.

A raccoon has a black and white face. It has bright black eyes, black fur around its eyes, and a pointed black nose. It has a line of white fur across its forehead and white fur around its nose. A raccoon has small, round ears. Its teeth are very strong and sharp.

Raccoons can make many different sounds. They growl, whimper, and hiss.

A raccoon has five long, thin toes on each foot. Each toe has a sharp claw. The bottom of a raccoon's foot has no fur.

Most animals walk on their toes. But raccoons walk on the soles of their feet.

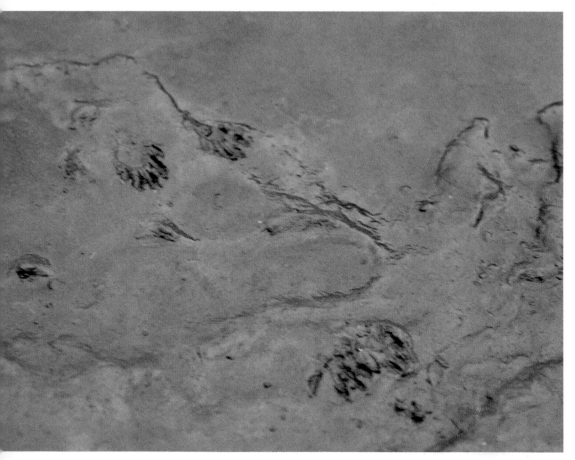

These tracks were made by a raccoon. Raccoons walk slowly. But they can run fast.

Each of a raccoon's fingers has a sharp claw.

A raccoon's front feet are called forefeet (FOHR-feet). Raccoons use their forefeet much like people use their hands. Raccoons can pick up very small objects with their fingers. And they can open things such as jars and doors.

Raccoons are very curious. They touch everything with their fingers.

Chapter 2

Raccoons are good swimmers. But they cannot swim fast. Where do raccoons usually make their homes?

Raccoon Homes

 Most raccoons live near a pond, lake, or stream. But raccoons can live almost anywhere. They can live in swamps or along beaches. They can even live in or near cities. The only places they do not live are on high mountains or in deserts.

Raccoons usually live in places where there are trees. Raccoons are very good climbers. They can climb big trees. Raccoons can climb down a tree headfirst or tail first. Few other animals can climb down a tree headfirst.

Raccoons live in trees or on the ground.

Each raccoon has its own home range. A home range is an area of land where an animal lives. A raccoon usually stays in its home range all of its life.

Raccoons usually live alone. But a mother raccoon lives with her babies until they are old enough to leave home.

16

Some raccoons live near cities. These raccoons usually have small home ranges.

Some raccoons have very large home ranges. They can be as large as 13,000 acres. This is about as big as a medium-sized town. Raccoons who live near cities usually have small home ranges. Their home ranges are as small as 12 acres. This is about the size of 12 football fields.

This raccoon lives in a den that is high in a tree.

Raccoon homes are called dens. A den is usually a hole in a tree or a log. It may be a hole in the ground where other animals once lived. A den can also be a small cave or a big bird nest. A raccoon may even have its den in a place like a barn or an attic. A raccoon usually stays in one den for a while. Then it moves to a den in another part of its home range.

Some raccoons live in places that have cold winters. These raccoons sleep in their dens during much of the winter. On sunny days they may wander out to look for food.

Other raccoons live in places that are warm all year. These raccoons do not spend as much time in their dens during the winter.

On sunny winter days, a raccoon may wander outside its den.

19

Raccoons often hunt for food in or near water. When do raccoons usually look for food?

They'll Eat Almost Anything!

 Raccoons have many ways of finding food. They have good eyesight, great hearing, and a good sense of smell. Raccoons also have a good sense of touch. They can find food just by feeling for it.

Raccoons are nocturnal (nok-TUHRN-uhl). Nocturnal animals look for food at night. Raccoons often hunt for food in or near water.

Raccoons are omnivores (AHM-nih-vohrz). Omnivores are animals who eat both plants and animals.

A raccoon spends most of the day in its den. It leaves its den at night.

Raccoons hold their food with their forefeet.

Raccoons eat almost any kind of food.
They eat corn, nuts, and fruit. They hunt for
crayfish, mice, small birds, and bird eggs. They
also hunt for crabs, clams, snakes, squirrels,
fish, turtles, frogs, and insects.

Raccoons who live near people look for food in garbage cans and in gardens. Raccoons even eat dog food or cat food from pets' bowls!

This raccoon is looking for food in a cooler.

23

Raccoons often dunk their food in water before they eat. People used to think raccoons wash their food. But this is not true. Some scientists think raccoons wet their food to make it easier to swallow.

Crab-eating raccoons aren't the only raccoons who eat crabs. Common raccoons eat crabs, too.

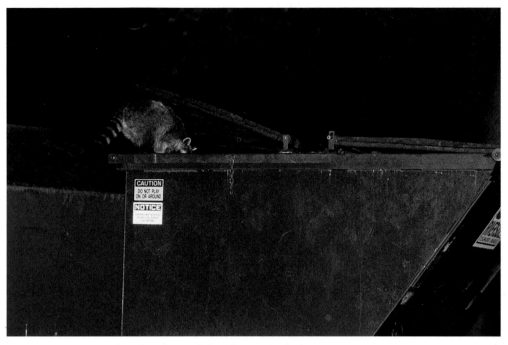
Raccoons may find a lot of food in trash bins.

Raccoons eat a lot during the spring and the summer. But in the fall they eat even more. They eat so much that they become fat.

By late fall, raccoons have a lot of food stored in their bodies as fat. They look like round balls of fur. During cold winters, food can be hard to find. But raccoons can live off their body fat. They can live through a cold winter without eating.

Chapter 4

A mother raccoon takes care of her babies by herself. How many babies does a mother raccoon give birth to at a time?

From Babies to Adults

 A female raccoon is ready to have babies in late spring. She looks for a den that is safe and quiet. Usually she finds a hole high in a tree. Sometimes the female gathers some wood scraps to make a bed for her babies.

A raccoon gives birth to about three or four babies at a time. Baby raccoons are called kits. Kits are about 4 inches long. This is about as long as a new crayon. Newborn kits weigh about 2 ounces. This is about as heavy as a plum.

Some raccoons give birth to just one baby at a time. But others give birth to as many as eight babies at a time.

Kits are covered with soft fur. Their fur is light gray. Some kits have no black fur around their eyes. And they have no stripes on their tail. Their eyes and ears are closed.

Kits have light gray fur.

Mother raccoons and their kits sometimes make purring noises.

Kits drink their mother's milk. They sleep a lot. They curl up together to keep warm. When they are awake they make noises. Sometimes kits sound like purring cats. Sometimes they sound like twittering birds.

When the kits are about three weeks old their eyes open. Their fur is longer. They have black fur around their eyes.

The kits climb around the den. They tumble and play together. They growl as they play.

Young raccoons are very active inside the den.

When they are eight weeks old, kits begin to peek out of the den. Sometimes a kit tries to climb out. But the mother picks up her kit by the back of its neck. She carries it back inside. She is careful to watch her kits all of the time. She leaves the den only to search for food.

A raccoon kit peeks out of its den.

But the mother cannot keep her kits inside for long. Raccoon kits are very curious. Soon they begin to crawl all over the tree that their den is in. Sometimes they fall asleep on the upper branches.

Raccoon kits explore on branches near the den.

A mother raccoon shows her kits how to find food.

When the kits are 10 weeks old, their mother takes them on trips to find food. The mother teaches her kits how to find food.

The mother shows her kits how to fish. She wades into shallow water. She feels around for fish. At first the kits watch her. Then they feel around in the water for fish, too.

A mother may push her baby up a tree to hide it from an enemy.

A mother raccoon also teaches her kits how to find insects. She shows them how to pull off a tree's outer bark. Many insects live under the bark. She shows them how to turn over logs and rocks to find insects, too.

The mother shows her kits how to hide from enemies. They watch and follow her. She also shows them how to climb trees.

When the kits are six months old, they can take care of themselves. Some leave to find their own home ranges. Other kits stay with their mother until spring.

Raccoons usually live about 5 years. Some raccoons live in zoos. These raccoons can live to be about 15 years old.

Some kits leave home by early winter. They look for their own home range.

Chapter 5

Mountain lions eat adult raccoons. What are animals who kill and eat other animals called?

Dangers to Raccoons

 Adult raccoons have few animal enemies. Predators (PREH-duh-turz) are animals who kill and eat other animals. Mountain lions are predators who hunt adult raccoons.

Adult raccoons are good at finding places to hide from enemies. But if they can't hide, they can look and sound very angry. They hiss and growl. They show the enemy their sharp teeth. And they fight if they have to.

A very angry raccoon can rip and slash with its claws and teeth.

Kits and very old raccoons have more enemies than other raccoons. Coyotes, wolves, and foxes hunt kits and old raccoons.

Foxes hunt kits and old raccoons. Large owls and dogs are other predators who hunt these raccoons.

Kits are very curious. A kit may walk up to another animal just to see what it is. Mother raccoons have to watch their kits carefully.

A mother raccoon defends her kits. If an enemy is nearby, kits hide behind their mother. The mother raccoon lowers her head. She hunches her back. She shows her strong teeth and screams loudly. Usually the enemy leaves. If it doesn't, the mother raccoon fights with it. She makes it go away.

Sometimes humans hurt or kill raccoons. Many raccoons are killed by cars. People hunt raccoons for their meat. And people use raccoon fur for clothing. Some people hunt raccoons as a sport.

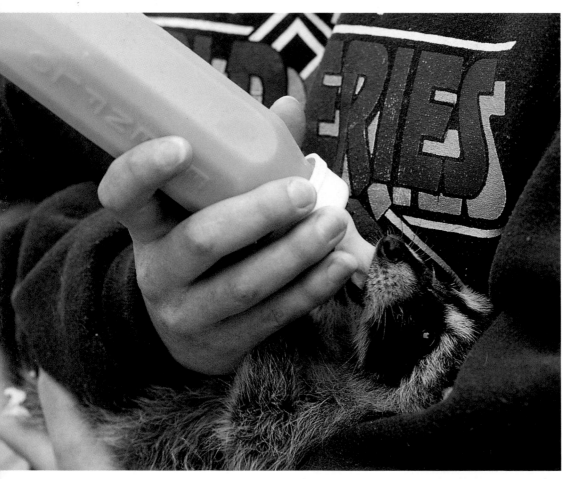

People sometimes take care of raccoons who have lost their mothers.

Raccoons look for food in garbage cans.

People have built houses and other buildings in raccoon home ranges. So more and more raccoons live near people. Many people think raccoons are pests. Raccoons knock over garbage cans. They scatter garbage all around. They open jars. A raccoon may even sneak into a house to look for food.

41

Some raccoons live near farms. They take food from farmers' fields. They may also take chickens from farms.

Raccoons who live near farms look for food in fields.

A raccoon rests in its den.

Raccoons are very curious and clever. They are clever enough to find homes and food almost anywhere. Maybe you have a raccoon living near you.

On Sharing a Book

As you know, adults greatly influence a child's attitude toward reading. When a child sees you read, or when you share a book with a child, you're sending a message that reading is important. Show the child that reading a book together is important to you. Find a comfortable, quiet place. Turn off the television and limit other distractions, such as telephone calls.

Be prepared to start slowly. Take turns reading parts of this book. Stop and talk about what you're reading. Talk about the photographs. You may find that much of the shared time is spent discussing just a few pages. This discussion time is valuable for both of you, so don't move through the book too quickly. If the child begins to lose interest, stop reading. Continue sharing the book at another time. When you do pick up the book again, be sure to revisit the parts you have already read. Most importantly, enjoy the book!

Be a Vocabulary Detective

You will find a word list on page 5. Words selected for this list are important to the understanding of the topic of this book. Encourage the child to be a word detective and search for the words as you read the book together. Talk about what the words mean and how they are used in the sentence. Do any of these words have more than one meaning? You will find these words defined in a glossary on page 46.

What about Questions?

Use questions to make sure the child understands the information in this book. Here are some suggestions:

> What did this paragraph tell us? What does this picture show? What do you think we'll learn about next? What are the different types of fur a raccoon has? How does a raccoon use its front feet? Where do common raccoons live? What is the area where a raccoon lives called? What is the place where raccoons sleep called? What do raccoons eat? Why do raccoons eat more food in the fall? Who are baby raccoons' enemies? What are baby raccoons called? What is your favorite part of the book? Why?

If the child has questions, don't hesitate to respond with questions of your own, such as: What do *you* think? Why? What is it that you don't know? If the child can't remember certain facts, turn to the index.

Introducing the Index

The index is an important learning tool. It helps readers get information quickly without searching throughout the whole book. Turn to the index on page 47. Choose an entry, such as *food*, and ask the child to use the index to find out what raccoons eat. Repeat this exercise with as many entries as you like. Ask the child to point out the differences between an index and a glossary. (The index helps readers find information quickly, while the glossary tells readers what words mean.)

Where in the World?

Many plants and animals found in the Early Bird Nature Books series live in parts of the world other than the United States. Encourage the child to find the places mentioned in this book on a world map or globe. Take time to talk about climate, terrain, and how you might live in such places.

All the World in Metric!

Although our monetary system is in metric units (based on multiples of 10), the United States is one of the few countries in the world that does not use the metric system of measurement. Here are some conversion activities you and the child can do using a calculator:

WHEN YOU KNOW:	MULTIPLY BY:	TO FIND:
miles	1.609	kilometers
feet	0.3048	meters
inches	2.54	centimeters
gallons	3.787	liters
tons	0.907	metric tons
pounds	0.454	kilograms

Activities

Pretend to be a common raccoon. Where do you live? What do you eat? What sounds do you make?

Make up a story about raccoons. Be sure to include information from this book. Draw or paint pictures to illustrate your story.

Visit a zoo to see ringtails, coatis, and other animals who are related to raccoons. How are raccoons similar to these animals and how are they different?

Glossary

dens: raccoons' homes

forefeet (FOHR-feet): a raccoon's front feet

guard (GAHRD) hairs: the longer hairs on a raccoon's body

home range: the area where a raccoon lives

kits: baby raccoons

nocturnal (nok-TUHRN-uhl): hunting for food at night and resting during the day

omnivores (AHM-nih-vohrz): animals who eat both plants and animals

predators (PREH-duh-turz): animals who hunt and eat other animals

underfur: the shorter fur on a raccoon's body. Most of a raccoon's fur is underfur.

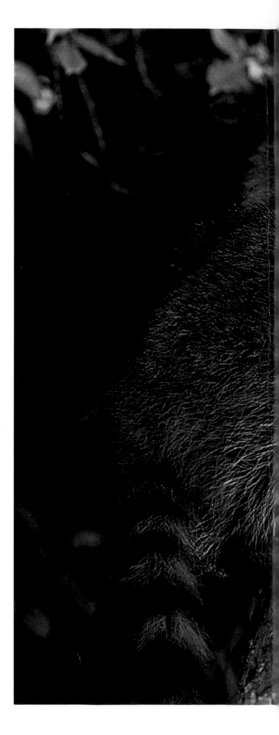

Index

Pages listed in **bold** type refer to photographs.

About the Author

L. Patricia "Pat" Kite is an award-winning children's book author. She has a special love for research—especially in the fields of biology and biography. Kite holds teaching credentials in biology and social science and a master's degree in journalism. She is a New York native but has spent the last 30 years in Newark, California, where she raised four children as a single parent. Kite's hobbies include gardening, reading, distance walking, local politics, and volunteer work.

About the Photographer

Jerry Boucher lives with his wife in rural Amery, Wisconsin. He has worked for over 30 years in photography, advertising, and graphic arts. His company, Schoolhouse Productions, does commercial photography, graphic design, and tourism brochures. The father of three sons, Boucher is also involved with Kinship, a teen photo group, and several arts organizations. He also teaches photography and drawing. His Lerner Publishing Group books include *Fire Truck Nuts and Bolts, Powerhouse, Flush!,* and *Rats.*